All About Me

My name is Elliot,
but my nickname is Racer.
That's because I'm fast!

My birthday is July 23,
and I'm seven years old.

I have brown eyes
and yellow hair.

My Family

There are lots of people in my family.

My mum likes to paint.
My dad likes to cook.
My big brother, Mack, likes to skateboard.
And my little sister, Ria, likes frogs!

My Home

I live in an old house
on Wood Street.

I have a pet rat
in my room.

I have a tree house that
I built with my grandpa.

My Friends

My best friend is Ben.
We like to skate together.

My oldest friend is Grandma.
We read stories together.

Toby is my friend, too.
We go running together.

My Hobbies

I like to go places fast.
I wear my rollerblades
or ride my mountain bike!

I like to collect things
like rocks and insects.

I collect stickers, too.

My Adventures

My family goes camping every summer.
We hike, fish, and swim.

My best adventure was when Dad, Ben, and I went over a waterfall!

My Goals

My hero is Toby.
He is good at running.
I want to be like him.

Some day I want to win
a great race.

Some day I want to fly
my very own plane.